TESSA RANSFORD is a poet, translator and literary editor. A cultural activist on many fronts for over forty years, she founded the Scottish Poetry Library. In 2001, she initiated the annual Callum Macdonald Memorial Award for publishers of pamphlet poetry in Scotland and has held Royal Literary Fund fellowships at the Centre for Human Ecology and Queen Margaret University. Full details of her work are available at wisdomfield.com. Recent poetry publications include: *Not Just Moonshine: New and Selected Poems* (2008); *Rug of a thousand colours* (2012), a collaboration with Palestinian poet Iyad Hayatleh inspired by the Five Pillars of Islam; *Don't mention this to anyone* (2012), poems connected with India and Pakistan, with calligraphy by Jila Peacock; and *Made in Edinburgh* (2014), reflections on Arthur's Seat and Holyrood Park, with photographs by Michael Knowles. *A Good Cause* offers a new selection of previously uncollected poems, the 'good cause' being ultimately the intrinsic good of poetry itself.

Praise for work by Tessa Ransford:

Rug of a Thousand Colours
...*a rich and meaningful exploration of what it is to be religious. It is human and it is raw. And these poems provide vital contemplations and comforts for a world in anguish*—LAUREN PYOTT, *The Bottle Imp*

Made in Edinburgh
The poems employ a large range of forms, but are characterised by lucidity and flexibility—TOM POW, *Scottish Review of Books*

Not Just Moonshine: New and Selected Poems
...*the fragility and complexity of life for humanity and in nature [are] themes which run through Ransford's poetic output*—IRENE HOSSACK, *Northwords Now*

By the same author:

Poetry of Persons (Quarto Press, 1976)
While it is Yet Day (Quarto Press, 1977)
Light of the Mind (Ramsay Head Press, 1980)
Fools and Angels (Ramsay Head Press, 1984)
Shadows from the Greater Hill (Ramsay Head Press, 1987)
A Dancing Innocence (Macdonald Publishers, 1988)
Seven Valleys (Ramsay Head Press, 1991)
Medusa Dozen and Other Poems (Ramsay Head Press, 1994)
When it works it feels like play (Ramsay Head Press, 1998)
Scottish Selection (Akros, 1998)
Indian Selection (Akros, 2000)
Natural Selection (Akros, 2001)
Noteworthy Selection (Akros, 2002)
The Nightingale Question (edited and translated, Shearsman, 2004)
Shades of Green (Akros, 2005)
Sonnet Selection with eight Rilke lyrics translated (Akros, 2007)
Conversations with Scottish Writers No. 3: Tessa Ransford (Fras, 2007)
Truth and Beauty (Netherbow Chapbooks, 2008)
Not Just Moonshine: New and Selected Poems (Luath Press, 2008)
Poems and Angels (Wisdomfield, 2011)
Rug of a thousand colours, with Iyad Hayatleh (Luath Press, 2012)
Don't mention this to anyone, calligraphy by Jila Peacock (Luath Press, 2012)
Made in Scotland: Poems and Evocations of Holyrood Park (Luath Press, 2014)

A Good Cause

TESSA RANSFORD

Luath Press Limited
EDINBURGH
www.luath.co.uk

First published 2015

ISBN: 978-1-910745-25-0

The author's right to be identified as author of this book
under the Copyright, Designs and Patents Act 1988 has been asserted.

The paper used in this book is recyclable. It is made
from low chlorine pulps produced in a low energy, low emission
manner from renewable forests.

Printed and bound by Bell & Bain Ltd., Glasgow.

Typeset in 11 point Sabon

© Tessa Ransford 2015

*This book I dedicate to my youngest grandchild, Dara,
born 29 November 2014*

Contents

Acknowledgements	10
A Good Cause	11
To remember or not	12
A sign for our time	13
The Floating Iceberg's Song	14
Dead statues	15
Crystal Ship	17
Belles Lettres	18
Let it not be said	21
Collie dog among the books	23
Hear, O Israel	24
Midas	25
Stock	26
Things mustn't go back to 'normal'	28
Is there a country?	30
The only	32
Cliffs	33
Religion among the people in Scotland	35
Religion in Scotland	37
Contumacious	38
The Cycle Path to Cramond	39
Deprived	41
The Enchanted Bridge	42
Mornings at Insh	44

Women's secret language in China	45
Rune for him	46
Rune for myself	47
Sheer Life	48
Rossal, Sutherland, in the mists of time	49
Disseveral Irish Couplets	51
Dundrennan	54
Pow Wow	56
Rescue Attempt	58
Glas fhairge	59
Not on the map	60
Camouflage	61
The Great Tapestry of Scotland	62
Raise	63
Epithalamion	64
Girls' song for counting cherry stones	65
Revelations	66
As I trod those stairs	67
Tea Ritual	69
beauty and freedom	70
Footlight	71
Adding to Favourites	71
For my grandsons	72
Lily of Raasay	73
Flos Campi	75
Barra	76
Chant, South Uist	77
but still a bird	78

Sentience	79
Aberlady Walk	80
December night, Edinburgh, 2002	81
Meeting of Gods	82
Rhymer's Glen, Abbotsford	83
Stromness Stroll	84
An Exotic Sanctuary	86
Turner in Cornwall	87
broken and free	88
Poinsettia	89
Indian Leaf Butterfly	90
Mantra	91
The Loving Spirit	92
For Eric Wishart at sixty	93
Tribute to Duncan Glen	94
Poem for Zena	97
The Shortest Day	99
Vale	100
Yeats's Grave	101
Marginalia	102
A Tryst	103
Trees for YES	104
Hope	105
Endings	106

Acknowledgements

Some of the poems in this book first appeared in magazines including *Chapman*, *The Eildon Tree*, *Fras*, *Gutter*, *Markings*, *Poetry Scotland*, *Scottish Affairs*, and *Sons of Camus*.

'Lily of Raasay' was first published in *The Thing that Mattered Most* (Scottish Poetry Library with Black & White Publishing); 'Things mustn't go back to "normal"' was published in *Adrian: Scotland Celebrates Adrian Mitchell*; 'Tribute to Duncan Glen' appeared in *Duncan Glen: A Festschrift*. 'Is there a country?' and 'Tryst' were included in *Scotia Nova: Poems for the Early Days of a Better Nation*.

For their help and support in making this book possible, I would like to thank Michael Lister; Iain Black, Richie McCaffery and Jennie Renton; Gail and Rod Shearer; my son and daughters and their children and partners; Henry Marsh and the group of poets who gather at Henderson's in Hanover Street; the staff at Luath Press and my good neighbours.

In 'The Great Tapestry of Scotland *a missing panel*', 'the grace that musicks us' is taken from *The White Noon,* a collection of sonnets by Iain Crichton Smith and was used in the first leaflet of the Scottish Poetry Library in 1982.

A Good Cause

Dew lies in the longer grass
spreading, bestrewing it
in graceful landscape of the level,
the parkland pretending to be tamed
or trying to be wild
wild anyway
dervishing with dew

Parnassus hill or Calton
I know which one I choose
as Burns would:
the one that bears witness to the hero
Thomas Muir
who devoted himself
to a good cause
the cause of the People.

Will it finally prevail?
Not while the New Town still
lays its upholstered values
on our systems.

Secreted, the Edinburgh I give my devotion,
hidden,
yet clear, open to the eye of the people
like the dew each morning.

To remember or not

Born into the start of the Second World War, I inherited
unspeakable pain that lingered from the First:
those who died, those who were spared, those who continued
bereaved, alone and bereft for the rest of their lives.

Memorial events and religiousness I do not enjoy
for how can I ever forget what surrounded me?
And how can I forget the nuclear weapons that lie
behind the lie in acts of official mourning?

My father's philosophy: Schweitzer's *Reverence for Life*.
He would never hunt or shoot or even go fishing,
he who had 'served' as a sapper and RE signals' officer
throughout those four insanely slaughterous years.

He loved life, was a graceful dancer and witty charmer.
He courted my mother for seven difficult years –
while she grieved her beloved brother and lost her youth –
yet together they cared for others in faith and love.

I don't need to keep on remembering that pain and clenching sorrow;
what I want is to stop the trade in war and armaments
that is still pursued across the world and sheds
more and more unspeakable pain through the generations

How can we say we remember and yet do this?

A sign for our time

Disgorged from a beached whale
Jonah gave warning to Nineveh
and that great city paid heed.

The whale itself came to London
on a suicide mission to save.
It struggled far up the Thames
level with Westminster.

Thousands gawked at the whale
a northern bottle-nosed beauty
and experts tried to save it.

They said it had lost its way
and wasn't too well. But it came to warn
that the planet is ailing and that
it is we who have lost our way.

The Floating Iceberg's Song

news report of an iceberg the size of Hong Kong floating past the African coast

Ahoy there, ahoy!
moored to Antarctica
over aeons
the rope broke and I drifted
away

no race round the world
I drip my ice-locked time
as I sail and melt

soon I'll swim in the Mediterranean
and block the Suez canal

my waters will flow as judgement
a mighty stream in the desert

ahoy there in the shopping aisles
and the shipping lanes

don't you see now

the planet floats like the Titanic in space
and can sink, can be utterly wrecked

Dead Statues

I'd willingly topple a statue
a Nelson or two could fall
from their sky-scraper columns
in a smashing pro-Europe gesture.

Wellington could be given the boot
or tossed from his prancing horse.
Kings and statesmen: time to depose them.
Burns, Ramsay, Sir Walter Scott
live in their work or not at all.
Let them escape their petrification
in eternal idolness.

We have no Joan of Arc;
we have war memorials in every town
where anonymous Woman is sculpted
as Death or as Victory.

Anonymous women with babies protested
against the closing of Elsie Inglis
Memorial Hospital, where she was
to be honoured in perpetuity.

It was boarded up and vandalised
then sold as a home for nursing the old
its gardens destroyed for more new homes:
homes for the well-to-do who
did nothing as well as Elsie.

Down with posers on pedestals.
Let's have a pedestrian crossing
yes, before a child is killed
and ramps to slow the violent traffic.
Let's put up swings, fountains
and sparkling roundabouts.

Crystal Ship

in response to George Wyllie's Crystal Ship

Crystal ship aloft the Clyde
transparent and electrical
quartz we know as magical
rock heart of our hard land

A ship for sailing to the future
vaporettos as in Venice
plying to and fro as ferries
embankments to have a dander

A massive question-mark is swinging
as the hook of an old crane:
Can we lift our loads again
build another kind of shipping?

Rock and water, sky and sea
let our journeys be strategic
out of car and drug traffic
into new community

Crystal ship aloft the Clyde
transmitter of a new message
connected to our old courage
catch the breezes, take the tide.

Belles Lettres

a poem constructed from family letters to my parents, in Bombay, written in Spring and Summer 1940

Three of my father's sisters, Ella, Isabel and Winnie, known as Jane, lived in Sussex: Ella in Arundel, and Belle and Winnie in a village near Worthing. Belle and Winnie moved in together to share expenses and because Winnie had to be evacuated from Kent. They were unmarried, in their fifties and sixties. Ella was newly retired from being a headmistress. Another aunt, my mother's sister, Phoebe, unmarried and in her forties, was stationed in and around London in the Auxiliary Territorial Service. The original letters are now in the Imperial War Museum in London, (DOCS.18875; LOCATION CODE 61/100/1)

Life is very grim indeed
planes drone over us day and night
roar like thunder din sans end
dodge between roofs in dogfights
siren blared
another raid
crash the roof, not a pleasant thought

180 downed on the Downs today
Nazis dropping out of parachutes
one fell half a mile away
Polish airmen, heroes of those fights
sudden a crowd
gathered who need
such excitements to keep up spirits
Winnie has come to save and share
on food, house, car and daily costs

She brought her pekes and 50 budgerigars
plus hens and pigeons, her gardening gloves.
Ella runs first-aid,
canteens, is head
of local voluntary efforts

Your parcel welcome of chocs and tea;
hard to write when we can't tell
if letter will reach you, or by sea
will take three months or more; church bells
will chime invasion
till then forbidden;
nightlong we pray it may not befall

Hard the silence all these weeks
Who is alive? Who disappeared?
You wear your heart out in war work
for troops and families displaced
evacuees
refugees
who is prisoner and who escaped?

We doze on stretchers on night duty
ready to organise a rescue –
bombs are destructive and dirty
the soot penetrates and overflow
from broken pipes and hinges –
the heart wrenches
a baby blasted through the window

We have made our wills; the evacuees
want us as guardians for their kids:
who knows if we'll survive? The veges
wither in heat these summer weeks;
we stand in queues
exchange news
the courage of folk, got what it takes

Whether Hitler comes our way or not
whether the yanks stop dithering and help
the Dunkirk epic gave us heart
how many saved in boat and ship
how many lost
the wounded cast
to die on the beaches without hope

How wonderful when you come on leave
when this is all over, one day soon? –
Perhaps to picnic or even bathe
go out to concerts, films again –
Winnie is ill
so what does kill?
We live in constant tension

Let it not be said

Let it not be said that I am indifferent to the consequences of immediate emancipation. I am indeed indifferent to them. I despise them wholly as put into competition with the demands which are made by outraged humanity for justice.
—Dr Andrew Thomson *(1759–1831)*, minister of St George's, Edinburgh, a passionate philanthropist who advocated in 1830 the immediate abolition of slavery, *regardless of the costs.*

Let it not be said
                that I am indifferent
to the slavery abolished two centuries ago
or the pleas made then by impassioned Scots –
such as Andrew Thomson aged seventy-two –
despite the threat of a total collapse
in the world's economy – and their own discomfort

Let it not be said
                that I am indifferent
to the arms trade that enslaves the world
manufactures war for the tools of war
to be sold as foundation for western wealth
our comforts, our freedoms, our cutting-edge science
our democracy and hypocrisy

Let it be said
                that I am indifferent
indifferent to any consequence
of the end of war and the arms trade
I despise them wholly when compared
with the widespread, outraged demand
for justice by humans among us

Let it be said
                through our knowledge economy
the networked consciousness of our species
our collective conscience, our international intolerance
of money from death   let it be said

regardless of cost, of cost to our lifestyle
of cost to our comfort, of cost to our tribe
of cost to our cars, of cost to our pride
it shall be abolished, the arms trade, now
regardless of cost

Collie dog among the books
Christian Aid Book Sale, St Andrew's & St George's, Edinburgh

Found a collie dog in the church
church is lost in a sale of books
books are sold for Christian Aid
aid to be sent for the humble poor
poor dog, an announcement from the pulpit
the pulpit where speaks the minister
the minister shepherd of his flock
and flocks of people buying books
books and some of them poetry
poetry and some of it Scottish
Scottish poetry can be found
found like the straying collie dog
incarnation of James Hogg?
James Hogg perhaps has just escaped
escaped from the John Murray archive
archive where his letters tell
tell of the humble Ettrick Shepherd
shepherd and dog lost, free and found

Hear, O Israel

An eye for an eye and a tooth for a tooth:
how many children, O Israel, do you kill
in revenge for an eye and
how many do you maim and starve
in revenge for a single tooth?

When Herod killed the children of Bethlehem
not knowing which was the one
the wise men worshipped
it was, and still is called
the massacre of the innocents.

It didn't succeed, for Jesus was The Messiah
which no brutality could prevent.
He advised us to love our enemies
and you know, O Israel, you know
your children will not be safe
unless you build justice and mercy.

Remember Amos, your prophet,
his simple practical message:
Seek good and not evil, that you may live.

Midas

in homage to Martin Ford, the Aberdeenshire councillor
who stood up to Donald Trump

Midas came hunting for something alive and beautiful
to kill by turning into gold.

His cloaked retinue were greed, arrogance and vanity
in the name of business, employment and prosperity.

The glare of gold had distorted their aim
and heavy shades masked the glint of cupidity in their eyes.

Roughshod over rough ground and shifting sands
they trampled a delicate ecosystem and local farms.

To build on sand is proverbially ill-advised
but concrete is good as gold for giant hotels.

A golf course, a gold course, a gold coast
clubs for the game and gaming for the clubs.

One man, not yet canonised, as he has to suffer first,
could take no pleasure in the prospect of such gold.

He cast his decisive vote against the will of Midas.
His eyes were open. He had no need of shades.

Stock

*The Oxford English Dictionary gives 69 definitions of 'stock'.
When it means a fund or store, the word evokes the trunk,
or stock, of a tree, 'from which the gains are an outgrowth'.
Collapse occurs when you prune the tree so heavily that it dies.
Ecology is the stock from which all wealth grows.*
—George Monbiot, Weekly Guardian, 24 October 2008

Take stock
make stock
root and stock
stock up
clear stock
stocks and shares

Stock the larder
stock the shelves
lock and stock
stock and barrel

Farm stock
herd and flock
choc a bloc
build on rock

Woodstock
tree stock
leaf and fruit
good stock

Cut and dock
now stump
now dwindling
now finished
shock
shock

Things mustn't go back to 'normal'
for Adrian Mitchell

After the war
people again wore collar and tie
hat and gloves
went to church, had Sunday lunch
minded their manners.
It was as if the rich and powerful
had simply been to a 'movie'
those four years.

It took the poets to do the moving:
remove the paraphernalia of privilege
shun the hypocrisy, abolish the ironing
the polishing and perming.

Thanks to Adrian and his friends,
to the poets and pranksters,
we can recognise sounding brass
and a tinkling logo.

After the banks collapsed
people again talk business as normal
with the hope they can again
play with imaginary money.

NO –

It is hard work –
from hand to mouth and mouth
to word from heart to head
and head to foot –
but for Adrian's sake let us
see that poetry moves us
and keeps on changing our lives.

Is there a country?

My soul there is a country my parents used to know
a country sore and sorry reaching for a better world
they humped the coal and cleaned the grate
they queued in shops and trudged the windy street
they hoped, believed, encouraged,
were witty, kind and good.

My soul is there a country now
which they would recognise?
The way we live more comfortably
with electronic systems;
the way we mix and marry and
swap our children round;
the way we travel freely
and communicate, no waiting
for replies, no longing, searching,
as there used to be, no aching;
cars and wars still multiply
with cruelty and stupidity
as we fail to learn, despite
the information revolution,
what we need to know for real:
what makes the commonweal.

My soul is there a country you may visit in the future
when women will be happy and playgrounds will abound
when animals are understood and sharing is rewarded
when jets have gone and juggernauts
cities are for local markets
when land is allocated so that all can grow some food
when learning is provided by those with skill and reason
and stories keep us wise,
the old are not neglected and the young are not exploited,
a world of human kindness
we do know how
we know we must allow.

The only

If you were the only girl in the world
and your world had collapsed around you
into dust, rubble, mounds, ditches,
all the people you knew vanished:
would you want a vote?

If he were the only boy in the world
and his world had been bombed around him
into dust, rubble, blood, bodies,
including his own limbs:
would he rejoice to be free?

If we were the only ones in the world
who knew or cared that the world
continue a home for humans,
for animals, plants, for life:
would we fight and kill?

Each of us is the only,
only us, only one world,
only our children, only
this chance, only a chance
if only now, all of us, now.

Cliffs

As we gather crumbs dropped
from the functional picnics of arts administrators
and festival directors and events organisers and
communication officers and public relations personnel

we smile and pretend we don't care
that we are a broken shell in their eyes, not even a pebble
on their beach, their oh so sunny beach
dotted with wind-breaker projects and
castles in the sand
funded to the depth where water is reached
resplendent until the tide comes in

all the spade-holders get their fee and their cheer
and who will care if next day it is all washed away?
They live for the moment in their shiny arts bodies
promising oh so many bums on the sand
or torsos in surf-suits taking a dip
catching and riding the trends

and oh so many international links
even if only flotsam and jetsam borne on the
commercial currents and marketing trade-winds
that need a safe harbour among previous
prize-winners and those seen on TV
with a nod and smile about their struggles
and dark periods

as we eat our crumb and continue our path
our truth-finder trail behind enemy lines
our daft but intense belief in our task
we reach those dunes, those cliffs
over the sea, clouds in the setting sun,
diamond air and birds calling

Religion among the people in Scotland

How far to Bethlehem? – not far –
we have to cross the frozen loch
and walk the moor
or brave the waves over the sea
to island shore;
we have to find a butt and ben
knock on the door

Is it far to Nazareth? – at hand –
we have to find the joiner's shop
the timber yard
or fish the seas and reap the crop
and work the land;
we toil in office or factory
long hours and hard

How far to Gethsemane? – don't tell
but it is everywhere you look
in the hospital
where folk will watch in pain and wake
and try to heal
and pray to be spared the quaich
or find the grail

Jerusalem, how far? – we know
all roads lead there if we choose
both high and low;
we walk beneath the needle gate
row by row
in poverty of spirit – faith
allows us through

Galilee? – walk by the lake
while sharing in the hardest task –
community;
we may be twelve, both men and women;
integrity
in daily life as loving human
our testimony

Religion in Scotland

In Scotland we suffer from religion
our religion is to suffer
unless we suffer we are not loved
by the god of our fathers

We don't do god as mother
we don't believe in nurture
we do not spare the rod
or the terrors of hell

In Scotland we choose to suffer
to suffer for the heathen
Mary Slessor, Eric Liddell,
to placate the god of duty

If we have a happy nature
we should call ourselves in question
something must be lacking
we will not be chosen

In Scotland we suffer for religion
it's our predestination
this life's a vale of tears
but not tears of compassion

* * *

Oh good folk of Scotland
sing and dance and play
you may be applauded
on destination day

Contumacious

The blast of the trumpet sounded our land
sent a glorious queen to the block and
women to follow the path of Martha
in medicine or nursing or teaching
cooking and cleaning

The Book of Discipline divided our land
whether to say the Mass with the French
or destroy our abbeys to please the English
and redistribute the wealth and estates
among a few powerful families

St Andrews a town of martyrs
fires to murder Hamilton, Wishart
and the cardinal lynched in the castle.
Golf and the academic life seem safe
but that horror and sorrow still haunt the streets

Covenants, statutes, confessions of faith
the articles for a new religion
which sought equality within its limits
but the pulpit was too proud for the spirit
and the beauty of ritual was driven out

No rule now but the golden rule
yet we make the golden calf our idol
money and influence with ignorance
of the guiding principles we fought for.
How shall we work our salvation now?

The Cycle Path to Cramond

Two set off one April day on the cycle path to Cramond

It took them through parks and by-ways
along cherry blossom avenues
braes and dells of leafy Edinburgh

Skirting Pilton and Stenhousemuir
they were joined by another
his bike battered and broken
who appeared to have come from Saughton

'We're heading for Cramond by the sea
with its Roman camp and ancient tower
where Almond flows into the Forth
by promenade and causeway
white swans and yachts
and a strand of black sand'

The third continued with them
on his rickety old bike
speaking quietly of a commonweal
to heal the ills of society
the need for peace and justice
care for the poor and hungry
in Scotland and the world

Despite themselves they listened
and in their hearts began to question
their previous unconcern

When they reached the inn at Cramond
tired now
the three sat down together for a drink
but the third drank only water
and blessed it as he did so

While they relaxed and chatted
their ordinary companion became less of a stranger

As he raised his glass
he was transfigured before their eyes
they saw him as their neighbour
our and every neighbour

Deprived

Poor Justin
 He can't
    travel except first class
    stay over except in a hotel

He can't
    be bothered with his children
    remember birthdays or Christmas
    imagine how others feel

He knows
    how to treat people as patients
    but not as equals or friends

He needs
    to be important
    to be the one on top

'others must learn to be disappointed'
he says,
a teaching he has refined

Poor Justin
    so clever
    so stupid
    so full
    so empty
    so rich
    and yes, so poor

The Enchanted Bridge

Thomas the Rhymer of Erceldoune
I have in mind.
He dwelt here after his sojourn
in fair Elfland
bound to speak only truth.
When his time came
to leave this life on earth
a white hind was seen
wearing a golden crown
in the main street of Earlston
where she stopped before his home.

A curvacious gracious mansion
stands by Leader Water.
Horses graze in circling meadows.
Ducks and hens and sheep with lambs
and dogs and more fine steeds
do not conceal the waly waly
imbalance of that demesne.

I have in mind the Faerie Queen –
and how she may be encountered
on woodland paths in the month of May –
when I find myself along that way
stony, mirky, leafy, flowery,
rainy, sunny, light and shady.

I trespass forward through the spinney
half wary that she might appear
or the poet himself with prophecies.
Her bridle bluebells spread the ground
but where her shirt of grass-green silk?

Beyond the brae and looking down
I see it stretched before my eyes:
a sward of green that forms a bridge
smooth, untouched and leading onward.

An old stone bridge across the river
arched and shaped with balustrade,
a sweet Mozartian composition
of elegant style, small-scale construction.
The water plays beneath in pools
wagtails flit, the dipper dances.
Someone stands with measuring rod
records dimensions, takes photographs.
He quietly tells me all he knows
true facts and figures of the scene
and of his quest to find this bridge
marked on maps yet strangely hidden.

This real unreal is interlaced
the Elfyn and the poet meet
where tracks are ever laid for them:
this bonnie road a requiem.

Mornings at Insh

You pause at the door you have opened
to taste the morning: sky for clouds,
trees for wind, grass for dew
as you clear away ashes, fetch logs.

You return and kneel at the fire
still barefooted and in your russet
pyjamas. You kneel in a kind of prayer
while working to coax a flame.

It is normal surely, and natural
but this is the ritual you have made
familiarly exceptional –
just what you have always done.

Another day is offered
the moment you open morning's door.
It rushes to every sense and asks
for response: 'Yes' – the word of flame.

Women's secret language in China

Secret language
for women, for only
women, mother to
daughter over and under

How we enjoy and how
we adapt, what children need,
when to hold on and
when to let go, what the body
knows, where we are strong,
why we live long

Renewable wisdom: endure,
listen, hear, wait, watch,
welcome, encourage, restore

Spindly signs like needle marks:
share, safekeep,
embrace, praise

Fury, mercy, laughter
will soon all die but
our language will
surpass itself

Rune for him

If your happiness brings another grief
you are a thief

If your happiness is another's cost
it will not last

If your happiness made you deceive
you will surely grieve

If your happiness made you despise a dream
it will be grim

If your happiness means destroying a lover
it will soon be over

If the days, weeks, months of your happiness
are another's calendar of distress

If you go up while another goes down
the pivot will turn

If you take good from another's ill
how can you be well?

Ride on ride on in your stolen bliss
till you take your toss

Grip the usurper close to your side
she is not your bride

The one to whom you truly belong
has been done wrong

This is a spell. This is a rune.
What is done is done

Rune for myself

This a rune I write for myself
to restore my health

The man who left in bitter sorrow
was but a shadow

The woman who snatched him in spiteful glee
will surely flee

Though he violently left me crippled and maimed
I shall be redeemed

Black with his troubles he darkened me
now I am free

With his skill and talent he despised mine
equally fine

For years he gave me love and torment
then he went

I have the truth of my endeavour
endures forever

My lasting diamond self remains
intact and shines

Sheer Life

Jesus I've worshipped again and again in the beautiful and young
but was he a gaunt prophet, even ugly with fasting and praying,
travelling and teaching, thinking and doing,
living and dying and living again –
for his goodness appears in the human through what is imperfect,
where weakness makes an epiphany in the fabric of flesh?

We are not like swans which moult and renew their plumage
year after year to look like disguised princesses;
in the human such sheerness is veiled except
in glimpses in smiles, in touches, in pain, in forgiveness.

The sacred is not constructed, intended
but can be discovered, created.
A lamb lies dead in the snow at Easter;
one more infinitesimal death, yet some angel knows
and we, however broken, must act as angels ourselves.

Rossal, Sutherland, in the mists of time

Black water deep in mist where sunless lilies gleam
mountains invisible almighty overhead.
Kircaig is crashing down and swirls on rocks below
where salmon river runs between banks of asphodel.

In tasteful Scourie Lodge the southern owners now discuss
palm trees cultivated, yet how salt sea spray flies
in the wind throughout the year to chasten plant and soil.

Here lived Evander, local factor for the Duchess,
Betty Sutherland herself, who demanded the wasteland
where townships and communities across strath and hill
stood in the path of 'progress' and desired modernity.

At Rossal a meadow a wide green acreage
long wet grassland smeared with sheep manure
and flecked with wool like litter, here beside the Naver,
a messy business walking around these humps and hillocks
where walls of what were homesteads, hundreds, lie revealed.

Patrick Sellar lived here who sold his soul
to the best modern practice and to the highest bid
and he cast the people out.
Now the very rock and stone, once a cause of hindrance
to plough and harrow, is in the eye of the prospector:
the people who walk in mist shall see another darkness.

Ossian lamented those who died defending honour
but how now for valour? a grant? some compensation?
There is promise of a job in buying and in selling
the Caledonian Shield, the oldest rock we know on earth.

The mountains will bow down and the sea will rise up
Dies Irae, Rock of Ages cleft for me.
Can we lift up our heads, lift our eyes to the hills:
the mist may even clear.

Disseveral Irish Couplets

A hare went by on the road in Kerry
Lippity-loppety, not in a hurry

Smart new homes with picture windows
television and soft potatoes

Farms grow vegetables and horses
or rather sell their fields for houses

The Old Red Fox, The Climbers' Rest,
Lord Brandon's Cottage; a swallow's nest

Kate Kearney's Cottage, ponies and carts
saddles parked on bonnets of cars

Climb to the cairn of the Celtic saint
St Finian, with his faithful hound

Folk leave coins in penance for sinning
others uplift them and go on drinking

Pass a Martyr's cross, 1923
roadside murder sets Ireland free?

Donaghue and O' Sullivan
Fionna MacCumhal and Garryowen

* * *

Fuschia tangled with honeysuckle
midges trapped in butterwort petal

Old coach road, the path to Mass
old railway turned to mud and moss

The sessile oak and holly woods
glen of the birches, the arbutus

Tiny black-winged butterflies
in ferny shadow of the trees

Mist and rain and swirl and sway
mixing forty shades of gray

Fog creeps in over Dingle point
McGillycuddyreeks grow faint

The priests, the puddles and the famine
a Cause for every occasion

The need for jokes, the dismal wet
reels and jigs and step-dance feet

glass design like jelly-fish
nature captured in a dish

A home you love, a life you hate
maybe have to emigrate

Then write to fictionalise the fact
Ireland will remain intact

* * *

Dark the water, dark the rock
dark the bog and the mountain lough

Black turf ditch on the Fenians' hill
sundew, orchid, asphodel

through Dunloe Gap a Pilgrim's Progress
the vale of shadow and water roses

A patch of green where sheep are white
a patch of blue sky and sunlight

Sheep on stone-wall eating berries
waterfall that protects the fairies

Ossian floats on a milk-white steed
but the girth must break before he's freed

Mysterious Derryconnaghie
rock faces marked for fertility

* * *

Patrick Casey's 'Ken Brinceen'
leaps with dolphins off Caherciveen

Between the devil and the deep blue sea
monks of Skellig's monastery

Perched like birds in stone colonies
building their cells and rock staircases

Climb the precipice, don't look down
pray for the puffins and campion

Dundrennan

Dreaming ruins of Dundrennan
conjuring the calm Cistercian

Overtopped by ancient trees
growing through the centuries

Arches branching intertwine
leaves with carving in design

Shapes of sunlit sky reveal
where shades of silent abbots kneel

The geometry of dark and light
lets past and present penetrate

Politics of prayer and practice
were sculpted into solemn business

Sheep and ships for vault and pillar
sheltering both church and cellar

Among the ruins of Dundrennan
skip the footsteps now of children

Summer-clad in chapter-house
all unencumbered with remorse

Their pilgrim parents tread the grass
where Mary Queen of Scots heard Mass

The gentle people of Galloway
took your unwanted stones away

They left your lonely lofty frame
the poetry lingering in your name

Pow Wow

Feathered child   butterfly
a-dance   a-stamp
a-prance   a-step
song and drum
throb and thrum

Awake   respond
heart of earth
pulse of life
to head and hand

the tribes process
sunwise round
as invocation
voices sound

Women   girls
dignified
link arms
motherhood

Beaded hair
silvery bells
moccasins
totem dolls

White Eagle   Black Feather
bounty flows from one another
Deerfoot   Foxfur
Heartroot   Wingspur

Feathered child   bonny fellow
Butterfly   shining eye
Tell anew the tribes today
Chippewa   Menominee

Rescue Attempt

Bundle of feathers flapping on the beach
a wounded bird – the sands are empty, wide
the black-backed gull alights alert to watch

Can we pass by? So near yet out of reach
the bird is struggling now beyond the tide
feathers black and white there on the beach

'A guillemot', is all the bird man's speech
as gently he approaches from the side
the black-backed gull still waiting on the watch

He strokes the head with reassuring touch
then gathers the sleek bird, sharp-eyed
sharp-beaked, wings flapping on the beach

He takes it to the water's lapping edge
and now it tries to swim and flow and glide
that black-backed gull still hovering on the watch

Glas fhairge
(A gray-green sea)

Don't build close to the shore lest hungry waves demand more
and seek whom they might devour on a wild spring tide;
in vain to buttress with walls, nothing like that forestalls
the surge that rises and falls, cutting deep and wide;
on a summer afternoon imagine the hurricane:
breakers crushing the town, flooding the countryside.

Birds and animals know by vibrations from below,
sense gales in a distant glow: they will move inland;
while we have to catch the ferry, get somewhere in a hurry,
biting the salty spray that spatters on lip and hand;
father and forefather foretold changes in weather
by cloud or leaf or feather: they could understand.

The sea is faithful and gray, reliable day by day;
let the children play on the rough and tumble beach;
white sails on the blue, cruise ships passing through,
trawlers come and go, but lifeboats launch and search
for submarine's mayday call or tanker spilling oil
or lobster boat in trouble they must try to reach.

And all the while we toss our industrial trash
even our nuclear waste into the global ocean;
we pipe out our sewage, fish-farm spillage,
the rubbish from the village, without the least notion
that the sea has its balance, its own precise substance
and performs a perfect dance in ceaseless time and motion.

Not on the map

My Edinburgh's no longer on the map
folded, torn with use over the years
new streets and houses spread and overlap

I use a magnifying glass perhaps
but something always somehow interferes
my Edinburgh's no longer on the map

It's not exactly that I find a gap
but that where I'm searching it appears
new streets and houses spread and overlap

Upside down? Open another flap
but as if to verify these fears
my Edinburgh's no longer on the map

Put it away – it is a visual trap
we lose the very precinct most endears
new streets and houses spread and overlap

Camouflage

Some birds aren't camouflaged at all
no point their trying to hide.
I watched the crimson cardinal
'look at me' he seemed to call
his black eye fierce and proud.

With stocky beak and cocky crest
all extrovert his carriage;
gray-limbered trees and moss-green marsh
a back-drop for his scarlet breast
the priesthood of his plumage.

When I'm in danger of the red
or when it seems revealed
I'll quickly cover it or shed
the suit of crimson, wear instead
just feathers of the field.

The Great Tapestry of Scotland
a missing panel

let's stitch one more
a missing panel

come help all you hundreds who helped to make it –
The Scottish Poetry Library
deft, central, integral
in Celtic weave, its logo:
flower   atom   wave
folk   work   place
skein   thread   needle
a cross-stitched heart
a rosa mundi of mountain and machair

when we opened the doors of poetry
like Blake's perception
not to 'people' but to ourselves
ours, us, our poems
to have and hold, to find and share
take and translate
the logo spoke its own word
in all our languages
the grace that musicks us

Raise

Raise
me from the pavement, from the gutter, from the earth
Raise
me from conception, through gestation into birth
Raise
me from childhood, from falling and failing
Raise
me from illnesses from sadness, nought availing

Raise
me from neglect, from feeling forsaken
Raise
me from betrayal, and from being mis-taken

Raise
me from remorse, from guilt and despair
Raise
me – until I am – aware

Raise me from the ego

Free me from the prison

I want to know I'm raised once more
to say – now I am risen

Epithalamion

All has been said
of love in Spring
what more can I add?

Yet springs this new Spring
and loves this new Love
each time a new thing...

new powers to prove
new selves to discover
new pathways to rove

and find a true lover –
this Life must require
repeated for ever...

but human desire
is to choose where we go
no longer entire

in knowing we know
the spirit-creator
insurgently moves

for we are the creature
who knows that it loves

Girls' song for counting cherry stones

Mansion, Cottage,
Cotton, Silk,
Poor Man, Soldier,
woman's work.

Highest, lowest,
Coach or Rags,
Farmcart, Tinker,
men are thieves.

For my daughter?
for myself?
Count each stone
that numbers life?

This year ever
never next,
no more waiting
no pretext.

Poverty, Pigsty,
Wheelbarrow, Satin,
rewards are only
in the eating.

Spit each stone
and chuck away:
*what shall YOU be
girl?* I say.

Revelations

I kept waiting for the fairy godmother
but Cinderella didn't know she would come

I kept avoiding the rosy apples
but Snow White was unaware of her fate

I wanted to wake up to new ideas
after the enforced sleep of my education

I waited too long before I knew
I was my own fairy godmother

I avoided the juicy fruit too long
before I began to taste and see

but I danced with new ideas again and again
and made up for those comatose years

As I trod those stairs

These stone stairs fill me with woe
gray, hard, dark and worn in patches as if
with tears not feet as if with
indestructible despair circled
settled on them from a time when
orphans trod them.

A pang came upon me
of childhood fear and loneliness despite
the trappings of the gallery its
servitors in uniform its
hush in large defurnished rooms adorned
with paintings pictures of slashed colour
large or smaller slapped on wood
exuberant yet trapped, layer on layer
revealed and framed but colours
leaking over margins and entitled
'memories' or 'rain' or someone's
somewhere garden.

I am surprised myself by this attack
which later cups of tea and talk could
not assuage. Where did it come from?
I was not an orphan, yet for weeks on end
I was, for years in boarding school.
The chill lies thick there in my body still.
How could it? What are stairs, is stone?
For me a sign of fear and being alone.

Colour can be caught too early
framed, prevented, even as it tries
to spill, escape the square of wood
the stairs of stone.

Tea Ritual

Two tatami mats form space
desired
for taking tea in Kyoto.
Thus confined, kneeling, hands upturned
in acceptance of life and death
the bowl is then raised, gently rotated
to reverse the passing of time
and the whirl on the potter's wheel.
Lips meet rim in sacred sip;
tea is tasted, pure, green from mountain slopes
below the snows, the moon
its tiny leaves temporal, eternal.

beauty and freedom

snail shells gathered over the years
are coming alive
beauty and freedom

chosen for colour and contour
kept in jars, glass dishes
glued to boxes for ornament
as beautiful objects

now they claim to be creatures
emerge with eyes on stalks
and trail slime on the walls

I recognise them from beaches and grasses
where I walk and play
stoop to pick that perfect shell
or a child presents it to me
to carry home in a sandy pocket

now hundreds of snails are coming alive
and escaping –
a child has brought a brass bucket
and is taking it into a garden
to spread them in heaps on the earth

may they quickly hide from sharp-beaked birds –
how one life devours another
and beauty is no protection

Footlight

Sun at evening
beamed so low it lights
the foot of trees
where they stand in coarse grass
while branches are in shade

Radically angelic
light
where we stand firm
together
bearing our branches

Adding to Favourites

What is our favourite in all creation?
Air cried, 'let there be breezes.'
Water declared for tides and wells.
Fire wanted new-found planets
but the goddess of *Earth* said 'let there be bees.'
Mother and child agreed
and the cowslip bells.

For my grandsons

Little Orpheus
how you sing the world
transform its colours into music
make its forms into songs
dance your eyes and hands
fling yourself from every frame
you climb
as if a fledgling
a merlin or a linnet

your will-power almost
too strong for your body
your love of beauty almost
too much for your eyes
your sense of rhythm almost
too much for your breath
the enchanted world you live in
must respond to your delight

Lily of Raasay

Lily of Raasay
gentle your growing
child of the islands
woodland and moor;
you will imagine
worlds for exploring
as you are stepping
over the shore.

Father and mother
comfort and hold you
their love is for you
better than gold.
Grant you courageous
sensible, kindly,
bonny and thoughtful
honest and bold.

Dark as the raven
eyes of the ocean
hazel and willow
wisdom and grace;
mountain and birch trees
above and around you
light of the islands
shines from your face.

Lily of Raasay
what can I more say?
Now I behold you
give you my words.
When I have left here
they will be with you
silently singing
for all my sweet loves.

Flos Campi

for my mother a year on from her death

I bless the seals who like my children come and go
how easily they exchange their element
rock to wave to wave to rock
in their violet viola seascape

I bless the haze of flowers
like Vaughan Williams' shimmer of chords
across the machair in strains
and *flos campi,* the orchid,
magenta, white and mauve
while *seilisdeir* by the lochan
play arpeggios of gold

Barra

The wind the tide the cockle strand
larks and plovers wheeling
a belt of flowers between the sand

the 'twin otter' keeling
round the headland over rocks
as if a seabird landing

a seabird messenger of gods
an angel taken for granted
while men with mail and luggage bags

unload load-up unhurried
the wind the tide the cockle strand
together and concerted

allow the little plane to land
where duck and seal play dive and seek
and swim and fly and seem to speak
of wind and tide and cockle strand

Chant, South Uist

Skylight   framed sight
skyview   gray blue
cloudscape   chord shape
windwail   atlantic gale
birdcall   sea squall

seagrass   kelp mass
haycock   seal rock
ring plover   bird lover
lapwing   gleaning
otter holt   idle boat
fish abound   seals around

wild ponies   old stories
black cattle   tune the fiddle
sheep and yarn   another one
interwove   peat stove
grind grain   endure pain

skylight   dark night
moon and stars   blood and tears
wet and cold   wings fold
sleep long   ancient wrong

walk the sand   hand in hand
song and dancing   water glancing
go away   one day
window   rainbow

but still a bird

as I grow old
I see the world
as if a field
with no pony in it

the water-trough
in an old bath
the stony path
the contour of it

the leaning branch
the muddy patch
the thistle swatch
surrounding it

his occupation
his habitation
his vegetation
hoof-marks on it

unponied field
unhumaned world
but still a bird
may sing in it

Sentience

Imagined music in wood-panelled rooms
'woman's love and woman's life', the boards

subdued rooms, small windows where
the pictured view becomes part of the prison

escape into the woods where narrow paths
encompass sudden sunkenness and roots

through the weathered gate they slope uphill
celandines attract me more than roses

discover a sundrenched corner or a bench
to sit and watch the bare-foot children play

or catch the rock that catches slant of sun
and lets it go again ecstatically

the watcher who remembers has escaped
has known the prison everywhere and none

Aberlady Walk

We meandered the path to the shore to the point
where a raft of Eider rides on champing waves
below the rocky bank

Lapwing and plover calling and redshank stalking
along the bay sandpiper and dunlin
beside the sea – at sea-level – a sense of being
balanced there walking
between the ocean and coast

The track led over dunes and marsh
through buckthorn and rose, rose
and orange the sun in the west
above cloudspread black
as darkness was gently embraced

Darkness, December evening
crepuscule
with curlew call through the non-seeing
and Venus was suddenly flooding
our eyes as thousands and thousands
of geese came wheeling in as they cried
calling, settling
time to be home

December Night, Edinburgh, 2002

The fox and the swan have come to town
I met them both today.
The swan was wearing her whitest gown,
flew over the park and swooped down
on leaves beneath a tree.

The fox was clad in a mangy coat
and hurried along the street.
In dark and cold he paused a while,
then set his face for the Royal Mile:
'I'm king of the castle', he thought.

I saw a tall house tumbling down
on South Bridge from the fire.
The Tron clock white above the town
while a full moon ghostly shone
through frosty dusty air.

Swan you do not want our bread
polluting your pond water.
Fox, throughout the city fed
from finest refuse bins, you need
accept no grace or favour.

The clock face hanging like the moon,
a weird Christmas omen;
the street is filled with brick and stone
and dusty spirals round the Tron
inscribe the angels' warning.

Meeting of Gods

A birch grows out of the rock
beside the waterfall.

Which is the strongest of these three gods?

Tree slits rock
rock gives water carriage
water feeds tree
tree shades water
water moulds rock
rock supports tree.

Each sustains the others
and depends on them.

Yet water is creator.

Rhymer's Glen, Abbotsford

JMW Turner in the Vaughan Bequest,
National Gallery of Scotland

secret haunt, a narrow burn
the willows and the birches
a clearing with a wooden bench
and late summer weariness
in even slender branches

trees protect the watercourse
the tumbles and the pebbles
they listen to its message:
topmost twigs make gentle dance
and leaves float on the surface

coolness of the afternoon
song of running water
sepia golds, a twist of blue:
True Thomas and the fairies
gossip in the grasses

vignette offered free in space
tiny stroke of walking stick
ordinary, organic:
here is absence both and capture
painted presence and departure

Stromness Stroll

Ferry at sunset and every sofa or seat immediately
clothed in a sleeping form, boots emerging
from draped coats; oil men who must be
on duty tonight settle in seats in the lounge
and seasoned commuters hurry for ketchup and chips.

A class-group of children, (Primary 5?)
are not tired yet from their excursion.
Soon they'll be welcomed when they arrive so
late and dark, wrapped against cold winds.
Next morning the vennel's turned into a stream,
the main street drenched but busy; the post lady
smiles, quite used to the weather, leaps
up steps and closes. I tack my course
to the south, the museum, where I fall
into daring adventures of sea-going lads
and explorers from Hamnavoe to the vast
expanse of arctic ocean and to Hudson bay
and beyond.

John Rae in his sailcloth jacket and beard
paddles his cloth-built canoe, intrepid
and tough from his Orkney childhood,
his determination laced
with admiration, learning
the skills of Indians and Inuits
who taught him how to travel the rivers
and snows, to hunt and survive.

Into the rain and wind again I look for
a coffee and find it after buying the book
Vinland by George to read on my long route
home to my eyrie opposite the hermitage
on Arthur's Seat, the high place, or the
Bear Hill, or Mountain of the Shi.

Sunday and yesterday's river is paved
with sun amid flurries of sleet. All change.
Mr Merriman's shop and Wishart's,
the heart's merry wish and 'deep caverns for divers'.
Folk play golf above the boats in the bay
or stand at the door of the Baptist Church:
a cleansing indeed, a dip in the world
beyond boundaries, and tomorrow
another ferry
back to the railway tracks of mainland life.

An Exotic Sanctuary

'She pierced the forms to contain colour';
Barbara Hepworth sculpture garden, St Ives

Spaces
    not empty
        but form pierced
to admit colour
    and more
        sea, flower, sky
verdant, ardent

Artists scraped at surfaces
    of paint, clay, slate
        bronzy wood or woody bronze
and of conventional life
even as they scraped a living

Fishermen's shacks as studios
    blazing sunsets and storms
        spirals, conversations
chisels, mallets, knives,
    tackle, tools, boats
waves of light and shade
search for the unknown colour

Water in curved 'river form'
and the baby in Burmese wood
expectant, new as the art

Stringed figure
cantate domino
Apollo in coiled steel
sphere with 'inner form'
mother and child
poised form

Turner in Cornwall

A saddle-bag with his sketch book
all he needed, wanted,
as he rode the granite coast
on a sturdy horse –
St Just, St Ives, St Levan
Mousehole, Minack, Morvah,
the quoits and coves and menhirs
in search of light and colour
how they tease and dance each other.

The sun rising through vapour
he caught on the cliff near Zennor.
Fishermen and boats
a touch of human toil
amid nature's turmoil.
Dayspring from on high be near
sang Charles Wesley
riding the same path.

Turner loved storm clouds –
Storm clouds at sunset –
though perhaps the horse reached
the end of its tether
turned its back to the wind.

And even in today's prettified life
I joined a group by the wall
gathered to watch the sunset
as it gloried the sea and rocks
wild over Porthmeor bay.

broken and free

glad was the cable to be trun-
cated, left hang-
ing out to cast a
curvy shadow
on the red wall
to hear the chatter and
feel a belonging for
the antique wooden chair
once painted blue.
I'm sort of free, she thought,
at least not nailed
invisibly
under the boards where
I was useful and joined up
but now am broken
and free

Poinsettia

Deep red, more of intelligence
than passion, a thought
process through every leaf
a tinge of integrated
self-belief.

Wine-red wild in Mexico
a ruddy shrub, all warm leafage
with the merest nod
to flowers in tiny apologies.

Indoor plant, blood-hearted
always on the urge of life
yet reserved and undemanding;
even when the red gives place
to green the leaves are shapely
and the whole is elegant.

A life then of the leaf
of intellectual passion
and of quiet rhapsody.

Indian Leaf Butterfly

Underwings brown and sere
tapered to a stalk
folded and creased
as a dead leaf
or a prayer

Opened wings reveal
bold blue and gold
black fringed
with white rings
and strains of purple in the paler blue
luminous, fluorescent

Prove in flight the inside
(or the out)
the back (or front)
when all seems dead and withered
hanging on

Mantra

Forepresences foreshadow and forebrighten
find or follow light, as slanting, shed
like sound when it illumines a vibration
a sign, a visibility of rhythm
new patterning within a thinking head.

To perfect, accomplish, all-embrace
the solid detail and the fleeting trace
the word that clarifies or at once enlightens
other meanings, happenings; our daily bread
all that nourishes *ce jour-ci*, is understood,
stands us firmly earthed on rock or wood
within the flow, encircling cataclysm.

The Loving Spirit

The loving spirit lingers long,
And would not pass away—Emily Brontë

Now she hardly speaks or eats.
It seems body has taken control
from brain in final reversal.

She knows there is little left
to say that we can take in,
nor can she digest our messages.

She needs another kind of kindness
such as the world and our dumb
choking helplessness cannot deliver.

'I want to die but I don't know how'
and her fingers pluck and cling
to the bedclothes, handkerchiefs,

our arms and hands. She can't let go.
'Don't be sad when I go' – No,
but we are, we are sad at the

long, drawn-out manner of it
as she kisses our cheeks and asks
'When will mother come?'

'Soon', we say, 'soon – and
we'll tell her you're coming.
God bless you darling, good bye.'

We turn, we have to go. We are crying.

For Eric Wishart at sixty

The threescore years in your account
itemise kindness, honesty, hard-work, humour
but under what column do we enter your
love of the different
the beautifully small
the overseas visitor
students
the Romanian orphan
Russian poems
Chinese philosophy
hopeful artists, hopeless writers
late-night-time-spent
biscuits, your old red windcheater
cycling, travelling on local transport
detecting books to lend to others
teaching, guidance, friendship
meeting for lunch?
May this world share you with us
for many more years to bring
joy and do good.

Tribute to Duncan Glen
for his seventy-fifth birthday, January 2008

If you are born with a love of books and have a brain in your head, I think you just do it.—Conversations with Scottish Writers No. 2 (Fras, 2006)

If you are born with a love of books – and
you were, Duncan, seventy-five years ago,
almost as if born with a book in your hand
or with a typeface inscribed on your brow:
a love that would at first hardly know
itself, would struggle to consciousness
to recognition, delight, a thrawn 'yes'.

I heard that a cradle belonging to Burns was found
in the loft of a farmhouse among your people,
and that rich Lanarkshire rural Scots was the sound
of your thought and speech as you played football
or helped with the ponies or started to read at school,
while *the brain in your head* made thoughts into words
and sent you for treasure to library hoards.

I think you just do it – read, write, explore.
You found the poems of MacDiarmid, a thinking rebel,
his mixter-maxter language, you wanted more –
to follow *Cencrastus*, the incremental
discoveries and then you turned to the practical,
the bibliography, not knowing where it was leading.
You turned up at Brownsbank, with the book you had written.

You printed pamphlets, believed in making things better –
and Scottish literature sagged in a sorry condition.
You gave it new life, in poetry, language, letter,
without self-seeking or personal ambition;
for *Akros* was shining, the conscious aim for perfection
which did not exclude, but gave a chance
to those who troubled to learn the steps of the dance.

Exiled for work in England, designer and teacher,
you did not dream of neglecting your Scottish roots,
but served Scotland, trusted its literature,
worked with Margaret unfailingly on *Akros*
as well as pamphlets, bibliographies, books;
and then you retired and returned to a Capital
which you enriched, even as it seemed ungrateful.

Duncan, how can I forget how you came to the rescue
of the Scottish Poetry Library's lack of design
giving us a distinction, flowing from you
in style and content, in aesthetic line,
when wit and seriousness with news combine?
With *Makars' Walk* and with delightful accuracy
you gave us the mark of experienced excellency.

As for me, you saved my poetic life
as once earlier you'd helped it on its way.
With Margaret, your intelligent, lovely wife,
you befriended me as a poet, published my poetry
among countless others in years of difficulty.
You wrote histories of print, of Fife and Lanarkshire
and poems have steadily glowed from an inner fire.

Illness tried to flatten you, Duncan Glen.
You even thought you might never walk again
but you did, and nothing, nothing ever can
destroy the literary work you have done
for so many over more than one generation.
Past and future will praise you, as well as your own,
who honour, respect and thank you, *John Atman.*

Poem for Zena
broadcast in *Soul Music*, BBC Radio 4, 26 November 2002

A motorway and rain
deep winter, deflected lights,
this going-into-darkness time of year.
Mahler's fourth symphony *adagio*
pleads with clarinets
protests with drums
and sustained lamenting cello.

Why am I forsaken?
Let me take comfort a little
are not my days few?

The good and the wicked
and the good-fun and the what-the-hell
and brown-eyed Zena
whose cup was kept at the brim:
we are all *poured out as milk.*

The music reaches my sadness
that my bright brave friend
faces death. She shines on
through the rain, her disregard
for her pain, her laugh as she listens,
her wise earthy comment,
her realistic decisions
and yet
her trust in people and
their resources, especially if
tried in the fire as her own have been.

Ewig... ewig... the Mahler refrain
echoes again,
music of persecution and
premonition, of at-one-ment,
kol nidrei at the heart
of things like life and death...

then a chord of triumph
bursts round the boxed-in car
as it speeds on into night.

The Shortest Day

Swans are flying and catch the sun
great white wings noisy with love

Gaelic is singing and catches the heart
an eala bhan
as if a voice for the silent swan
bearing music through generations
of isolation and exile and war,
ceilidhs, communities, new and old

What am I but another bearer
a swan, a voice with Macalister chords
born in the Asian dust
an ambassador hidden in Scotland
from here, from nowhere to wherever the world –
words, works, bonded and winged?

Vale

On Glasgow Central Station she saw him lift his hat

for my lifelong friend Catherine

Glasgow Central Station
sleeper train to London
away to seek their future

days of smoke and steam
girls are leaving home
adventure in their hearts

looking from the windows
those discarded childhoods
of parents on the platform

the night-train pulling out
left clutched in the hold
lonely and cold

in lawyer's bowler
dignified, bereaved again
his only child
his hat

and dark tweed winter-coat
her father stood
she saw him bid adieu and lift

Yeats's Grave

I trod softly to see your grave
I found it stark and bare
with gray gravel and blue headstone
beneath the cloths of heaven

A few dead flowers wrapped in plastic
were no embroidery.
The church standing at attention
seemed lacking in courtesy

We may be sure the Priest, the Levi
the Pharisee will pass by
and that the Good Samaritan
will not be on horseback

I wanted to spread out my scarf
for you, a make-do cloud
light and dark in gray and white
but the cold eye forbade

Marginalia

the swallow of Ballylee, Yeats's tower near Gort

We heard voices of war and poetry
friendship, death, love
in the four-square tower of the winding stair

The bedstead stacked with shelves we saw
and views from desk or battlements:
millpond, trees, stars

Broadsheets, photographs on walls
abandoned nest in a turret room
at narrow neck of the spiral stones

But remembered is the living swallow
nesting on top of tall blue curtains
like ornament in the Book of Kells

The bird peeped down on us ambulators
as if commenting on the commentary
then hopped along the rail and chirped
in exercise for flight

A Tryst

I used to walk down the Canongate, empty and dark,
after another day at the Poetry Library
whose very existence depended on my work
however exhausted I was, drained and hungry;
but I had a tryst to keep with Scottish poetry;
and I'd compare myself to my seafaring ancestor
who sailed to Australia in a Clyde paddle-steamer.

If he overcame the dangerous currents and oceans,
attacks by pirates and running out of fuel,
I could surely sail on with minimum funds
when I had a chart, a vision and a goal
with a volunteer crew of experts, friends and faithful
navigators; like ancient Celtic adventurers
we set afloat a curragh of poetry practitioners.

Such risk in action brings its accompaniment
and gathers its own momentum and impetus.
To wait and see or slump in bewilderment
will never achieve our destiny, our bliss.
To make our own decisions and choose our course
will see us voyage ahead on a life of adventure
and find our way to what next desirable harbour?

Trees for YES
26 August 2014

trees are rustling trees are talking
swaying saying speaking breezing
ceaselessly whispering yes of course yes
'aye' they keep uttering 'sure' they keep muttering
yes for sure sure for yes
rustling chattering dancing singing
trees for YES

Hope

We lost the referendum but we didn't lose
Hope.
Our hope was to win independence
and that continues.

The goal does not change
though tactics may.
Some of the players are resting
and new teams form.

I was injured on 22nd September –
and knocked out of play.
So now I watch others take action
and can support only in thought.
But thought is also deed.

Hope
Yes
Hope
ever beyond, and beyond itself.

Endings

Teddy is old
his head lolls
his stuffing has sagged
his grunt has gone
his nose is torn

I've thrown him away
today
out of kindness
for he cannot look forward
to dying

Luath Press Limited

committed to publishing well written books worth reading

LUATH PRESS takes its name from Robert Burns, whose little collie Luath (*Gael.*, swift or nimble) tripped up Jean Armour at a wedding and gave him the chance to speak to the woman who was to be his wife and the abiding love of his life. Burns called one of the 'Twa Dogs' Luath after Cuchullin's hunting dog in Ossian's *Fingal*. Luath Press was established in 1981 in the heart of Burns country, and is now based a few steps up the road from Burns' first lodgings on Edinburgh's Royal Mile. Luath offers you distinctive writing with a hint of unexpected pleasures.
Most bookshops in the UK, the US, Canada, Australia, New Zealand and parts of Europe, either carry our books in stock or can order them for you. To order direct from us, please send a £sterling cheque, postal order, international money order or your credit card details (number, address of cardholder and expiry date) to us at the address below. Please add post and packing as follows: UK – £1.00 per delivery address; overseas surface mail – £2.50 per delivery address; overseas airmail – £3.50 for the first book to each delivery address, plus £1.00 for each additional book by airmail to the same address. If your order is a gift, we will happily enclose your card or message at no extra charge.

Luath Press Limited
543/2 Castlehill
The Royal Mile
Edinburgh EH1 2ND
Scotland
Telephone: +44 (0)131 225 4326 (24 hours)
email: sales@luath. co.uk
Website: www. luath.co.uk

Not Just Moonshine: New and Selected Poems
Tessa Ransford
ISBN: 978-1-906307-77-6 PBK £12.99

This book celebrates Tessa Ransford's work over the last four decades. The selection draws attention to the authenticity and emotional integrity in her writing, her lightness of touch and openness to ideas and the world around her. The development of Tessa's style and technique becomes clear through the recurrent themes of her poetry; motherhood, destiny, nature and love.

Don't Mention This to Anyone: Poems and Prose Fragments of a Life in the Pubjab
Tessa Ransford
ISBN: 978-1-903373-18-2 PBK £8.99

Inspired by the rediscovery of an Urdu phrasebook, Tessa takes the reader on a journey to explore the differences between 'then' and 'now', linking the reader to a world now lost to most. These poems question what it is to be both British and Indian, drawing on the author's memories and experiences to celebrate and uncover an 'Indian' self.

Made in Edinburgh: Poems and Evocations of Holyrood Park
Tessa Ransford. Photographs: Mike Knowles
ISBN: 978-1-908373-84-7 PBK £9.99

For the last 30 years, poet Tessa Ransford has lived in view of Arthur's Seat and Holyrood Park. Drawing on the paradox of variety within stability as the landscape changes, yet remains constant, over the years and seasons, Ransford has built up this collection over many years in response to the view from her window. The beautifully descriptive poetry is accompanied by full colour photography throughout.

Scotia Nova: Poems for the Early Days of a Better Nation
Eds Tessa Ransford and Alistair Findlay
ISBN: 978-1-910021-72-9 PBK £7.99

A better Scotland is not only possible but necessary. Scotland's artists and writers have long cultivated a distinct and independent cultural tradition undimmed – indeed frequently provoked – by political union. The project remains unfinished as the country heads towards totally unprecedented territory. This collection of poems explores the possibilities for the future of Scotland.